**WingMan Books by
Christine Thomas Doran**

Maddie's Choice

Choose Life

Zephyr, the Dragonslayer

**Other Books By
Christine Thomas Doran**

Flash and Fancy An Otter Adventure on the Waccamaw River

Flash and Fancy More Otter Adventures on the Waccamaw River Book Two: Saving the River

Flash and Fancy More Otter Adventures on the Waccamaw River Book Three: A Dolphin Rescue

Tabby Kittens at Midnight

Choose Life

❧

Christine Thomas Doran

Choose Life
Copyright © 2019
Christine Doran

All rights reserved.
This publication may not be reproduced, stored in
a retrieval system, or transmitted in any form, recording,
mechanical, electronic, or photocopy, without written
permission of the author.
The only exception is brief quotations used
in book reviews.

Comments
flashandfancy@gmail.com

Illustrated by
Bob O'Brien

ISBN:

Paperback   978-1-950768-03-5
Hardcover   978-1-950768-04-2

Published by Prose Press
Pawleys Island, SC 29585
proseNcons@live.com

WingMan Books, is a division of
Addiction Resource Systems, Inc..
Dedicated to educating
children of all ages about the hazards of
addiction and addictive behavior.

addictionresourcesystems.com

zaddiction.com

Dedication

My book, Choose Life, is dedicated to not only the children in my family but to all children everywhere. My hope is that you will all make wise choices and always have the courage to be true to who you are.

May you all be Dragonslayers!

They Are the Wingmen

They are the Wingmen, always unselfishly there,
In your darkest hour, know that they care.

They share in your suffering and show you compassion,
Steadily supportive until victory's won.

They're the unsung heroes who hear your fears,
When you cry out in agony and pour out your tears.

They are family, friends, and teachers that you hold dear,
They are doctors and counselors, forever near.
They are the Wingmen who always encourage, never fear!

They are the Wingmen forever full of hope,
They'll give you the tools to help you cope.

Wingmen- comforting angels with their wings they will cover,
Loving arms they will hold you when the enemy hovers.

They are the Wingmen!

By: Christine Thomas Doran

Acknowledgements

A very special thank you to Bob O'Brien who has worked tirelessly on my Wingman Project books. As always, working with Bob has been a very rewarding experience, especially on a project that touches us to our core.

I also want to thank all the other Wingman Project people who are working behind the scenes to make this project become a reality. A big thank you to all the other passionate authors who are dedicated to a project that involves educating our children and in helping people who are suffering from addiction.

Thank you to my husband, Tom Doran, who has been beyond patient toward me. Thank you for all your advice and support in my writing efforts!

Last but not least, I would like to thank my sister, Nita Brady, for much inspiration she has given to me through her writing of the Dragonslayers Club book! She has helped to open my eyes to the crucial topic of the children of the incarcerated and to the cycle of addiction that is destroying so many families in our country today. Yes, we are in a crisis!

A glorious sunny day greeted Ethan on his first day of spring break. Feeling exhilarated, he got out his bright blue board and decided to skateboard over to his best friend Tyler's house. The smooth feeling of his ride, as he zoomed along the maze of sidewalks, made Ethan feel like a surfer catching the perfect wave.

"Freeeedom! No school for a week! No homework!" he yelled aloud into the blueness of the morning sky. Ethan expertly glided up the sidewalk to Tyler's house and was soon knocking at his best friend's front door.

Immediately, Tyler swung the door open. "Hey, buddy! What's up?" greeted Tyler with an enormous smile and a fist bump.

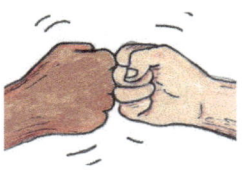

Ethan excitedly answered, "Hey, dude! You want to go surf the streets?"

"Oh yeah! Cool! Let me go ask my mom," replied Tyler eagerly. A minute later, Tyler emerged from his house with his new bright red skateboard tucked tightly under his arm.

"Wow! Cool board, Tyler!" Ethan said with admiration.

Tyler grinned, "Thanks! It's a birthday present from my dad."

"Be careful out there, boys!" warned Tyler's mom, who sounded very far away as he closed the front door. The fast friends were like two deer as they swiftly bounded off the three front porch steps.

Within the next minute, the two ten- year- old boys were surfing the sidewalks of the tree-lined streets of their little town. A look of joy shone from their eyes as they expertly zig-zagged their way through the neighborhood. "Freeeedom!" they both yelled at the top of their lungs.

Eventually, the boys approached the small- town park. Ethan and Tyler had been playing in this park as long as they could remember. When they were younger, their parents had come with them to watch over them carefully as they played on the swings and sliding boards.

Nowadays, they loved to come to the park because it had an amazing area of skateboard ramps where they could practice their jumps. Since they were older now, their parents trusted the boys were old enough to go there by themselves for a short while.

As they glided easily into the park area, Ethan and Tyler decided to sit upon a park bench for a short break. Ethan asked Tyler, "Are you going anywhere special over spring break?"

Tyler replied with a shrug, "Not really. I think we'll probably go to the beach. What about you?"

"Same here, but the beach can be pretty fun. I'm going to try out my new surfboard!" said Ethan. Surfing the ocean was just as exciting as surfing the streets to him!

About this time, the two friends noticed a teenaged boy appear from the nearby woods. He was walking in their direction, and as he got closer, Ethan recognized him as a kid named Jake. He had once been a friend of his older brother, Alex. At one time, Jake had been his high school's star quarterback.

"Hey, kids! What's up?" the teenager asked, avoiding their eyes. He was wearing a dark hoodie which partially covered his face. He looked at the ground and all around him suspiciously, checking to make sure that no one else was around. In his right hand he was carrying a dirty old black backpack.

"Oh… hi, Jake," Ethan hesitated as he answered. "What are you doing here?" Ethan knew that Jake had been into drugs with his brother, Alex, and wondered why he was in the park… and talking to them.

"Wanna see something really cool?" Jake asked, still not looking directly at them as he spoke.

"Well… I don't know. It depends. Like what?" Ethan responded.

Tyler chimed in and asked doubtfully, "Yeah! Like what?"

Jake pulled out of his backpack some little colorful packets. They looked like candies the boys were familiar with. Then the teen said, "If you open these up, you will find some amazing

candy that will make you feel really, really good, and then poof, all your problems will vanish away."

A look of doubt and suspicion passed between Ethan and Tyler. They were both wondering if these candy looking pills were really drugs and not candy. Having heard something about pills like these from the teachers at school, the boys were wary. If these were actually drugs, they were not the good kind of drugs they took when they were sick. Ethan started to have a very bad feeling about this situation with Jake.

Ethan was aware of how bad drugs could be. His older brother, Alex, had chosen to take drugs. His parents had noticed some changes in his brother's behavior. Alex had started hanging around with a new group of friends and quit spending time with friends he had once been close to. At school, his once good grades had started to drop. Then, Alex had even started to get complaints from teachers about his misbehavior in class. He had been arrested about a year ago by the police in the middle of the night. A loud pounding knock on the front door had awakened and scared the whole family. Alex was now getting help in a special place called a drug rehabilitation center. So, Ethan had seen firsthand the harm and hurt drugs had caused to his brother and to his whole family as well.

Suddenly, Ethan heard a mysterious still small voice whispering into his ear. He had heard it before when

he was about to make an important choice or decision. Ethan called this still small voice his Wingman, much like a guardian angel.

The voice of his Wingman said firmly, "Hi there, Ethan! Beware! Jake has bad, bad drugs that you and your friend do NOT need! You are smarter than that. Those kinds of drugs can damage your brain, heart, and other important organs in your body. They will fog your thinking. You can get addicted to them, and they will destroy your future dreams and goals, Ethan! Those drugs will make you do stupid or even dangerous things that can hurt you or other people. They could even kill you! Listen to me! I am always here to help you! Choose life! Be a dragonslayer!"

Ethan knew that the Wingman was right. He was glad he was there to remind him of how bad drugs really are. Facing his friend, Ethan whispered a warning, "Tyler, I know Jake has extremely bad drugs."

Tyler nodded his head to show that he knew this, too.

At that moment, another tall teenager emerged from the woods and walked in their direction. He was wearing a black jacket and had a black backpack, similar

CHOOSE LIFE

to the one Jake had, slung over his shoulder. Jake spoke to him as someone he knew well, "Hey, Paul. What's goin' on?" The two teenagers whispered something and then quickly exchanged some clear baggies.

The drugs they were holding reminded Ethan of an evil fire-breathing dragon. "I want to destroy you by taking over your mind and body!" the dragon of drugs roared as flames shot from his mouth.

Ethan looked at Jake and his druggie friend. "Uh, no thanks!" Ethan stated with emphasis. "I don't need those nasty little pills to feel really, really good. I don't need fake junk like that in my body to make all my problems go away!"

Tyler sighed impatiently, "Hellooo! Can't you hear us? No way! We're not interested! Duh… get it?"

"Aw, c'mon you little punks. You can trust us! It'll be so much fun! It'll be better than being on spring break! Ha! Ha! Ha!" mocked Paul.

Rolling his eyes, Ethan shouted, "How many times do we need to tell you guys? The answer is 'no way,' okay? What's your problem?"

"Come on, Ethan," replied Tyler, who was beginning to feel very uncomfortable. "Let's get away from these losers."

Ethan was beginning to feel anger building up inside of him. Again, he shouted at Jake and Paul, "You can't tell us what to do! You guys must think we're really dumb!"

Paul snarled, "What a couple of wimps! You're the losers! Go ride your stupid baby skateboards, you dummies!" The contorted faces of Jake and Paul as they jeered at the boys made the druggies look like demons.

Again, Ethan was reminded of the dragon that seemed to breathe out flames of anger fueled by drugs. It was a pretty scary scene, but he and Tyler refused to give in to the bullying pressure of Jake and Paul.

So, Ethan and Tyler turned their backs on the teenagers and walked away from what could have been a very dangerous trap. At that precise moment, Ethan again heard his Wingman whisper into his ear. He heard it just as clearly as the gentle rustling of leaves in the wind.

"Good job, boys," the Wingman whispered. "Always stay true to who you are. Choose life! Be dragonslayers!"

Soon, the two young friends were away from the teenage drug pushers at the park. Before they hopped onto their skateboards, Ethan and Tyler discussed the dangerous incident that they had just come face to face with.

Tyler stated with relief, "Whew! Those guys are such losers. I sure hope they straighten out their lives before it's too late."

Looking back over his shoulder, Ethan noticed the two teens were still standing in the same place where they had been before. He sighed deeply, "I hope they straighten out, too. I wonder at what point they decided to do drugs. But, there's still hope if they really want to change. You know about my brother, Alex, being in rehab, and all. He's trying to turn his life around, and I think it's working."

"That's great, Ethan! I believe Alex is going to be okay

with the help he's getting. That's awesome!" said Tyler. He had heard his parents discussing Alex in hushed tones, and he knew his friend must be very worried.

Then, Ethan turned to his friend with wonder in his voice, "You know, Tyler, when we were talking to Jake and Paul, I heard this little voice whisper into my ear. I call him my Wingman."

Tyler looked at Ethan with eyes as large as saucers. He said in a low, amazed voice, "Whoa! That's kind of weird, Ethan. What did he say?"

Ethan replied slowly, "Well, first he said that those guys had bad drugs that could seriously hurt us. Next, he said to always stay true to who you are. He said to choose life! Finally, he said one more fantastic thing!"

"Tell me! What?" exploded Tyler, flailing his arms as he spoke.

Ethan whispered as if he were telling a secret, "The Wingman said, 'Be a dragonslayer!'"

Tyler asked, in a puzzled voice, "Dragonslayer?"

"Well… see Tyler, every time I saw Jake and Paul, I imagined that the drugs they had were like an evil fire-breathing dragon ready to hurt or even kill you," explained Ethan. "The Wingman knew that, too, so that's why he said to be a dragonslayer."

Tyler exclaimed, "That's not weird! That's cool! We're dragonslayers!"

Suddenly, Ethan had an awesome idea. "Hey, Tyler. Why don't we, as dragonslayers, make a pact to never do drugs."

"Yes! I don't ever want to ruin my life by doing stupid drugs," Tyler said seriously.

So, right there at the edge of the park, the ten- year-olds made a promise to themselves and to each other to never take drugs. Into Ethan's head popped these words. He asked Tyler to raise his right hand and to repeat after him: "I, as a dragonslayer, do solemnly pledge to myself and to my best friend to never, ever, do drugs that will harm my mind or my body. I choose life! Dragonslayers rule!"

"Wow, Ethan! How cool is this! Dragonslayers rule!" said Tyler excitedly, who very much admired his friend.

Then Ethan said seriously, "You know, Tyler, I think we should tell our parents about Jake and Paul hanging around the park like that. What if they offer drugs to other kids who aren't as smart about drugs as we are?"

"Yeah, I agree," said Tyler. "What if some kids ended up dying! We need to tell!"

The two best friends fist bumped, jumped on their colorful skateboards, and happily skated off into the direction of their homes. They were both thankful for the Wingman, who they knew would always have their backs. What could have been a disastrous day had turned into a day of great joy and promise for the future.

Remember: "Dragonslayers rule!"

WingMan Books
Available at some local stores
and all on-line outlets

CHILDREN'S

WingMan Chronicles 1 - Spike,
Christine Medicus and Bob O'Brien

WingMan Chronicles 2 - WingMan,
Christine Medicus and Bob O'Brien

Joyous Jayden, Christine Medicus

Billy the Bully Two, Pat David

The Bunny Who Lost His Way, Nita Brady

Zephyr, the Dragonslayer, Christine Thomas Doran

PRE-TEENS/TEENS

The Dragon Slayers Club, Nita Brady

Choose Life, Christine Thomas Doran

I Am Fixed, Pat David

Maddie's Choice, Christine Thomas Doran

ADULT

Witness, Lee W. Hollingsworth

Misinformed Hearts, (Screenplay), Beverley Gadarda

SCHOOLS and COUNSELORS

The Dragon Slayers Club, Nita Brady

WINGMAN
Break Free - Stay Free

WingMan Books, is a division of
Addiction Resource Systems, Inc..
Dedicated to educating
children of all ages about the hazards of
addiction and addictive behavior.

addictionresourcesystems.com
zaddiction.com/

www.ingramcontent.com/pod-product-compliance
Lightning Source LLC
Chambersburg PA
CBHW041322110526
44591CB00021B/2879